W9-BGY-731

Very Simple
ARABIC
INCORPORATING
Simple Etiquette in
Arabia

Very Simple
ARABIC

<blockquote>
INCORPORATING
</blockquote>

Simple Etiquette in Arabia

Written and illustrated

by

James Peters

STACEY INTERNATIONAL

VERY SIMPLE ARABIC
incorporating
Simple Etiquette in Arabia

Published by
Stacey International
128 Kensington Church Street
London W8 4BH
Tel: 0207 221 7166; Fax: 0207 792 9288
E-mail: marketing@stacey-international.co.uk
Website: www.stacey-international.co.uk

© Stacey International & James Peters 2004

Simple Etiquette in Arabia first published 1977;
reprinted 1979 & 1981

Very Simple Arabic first published 1980

Fully revised combined edition first published 1994
Reprinted 1995, 1997, 2000, 2003, 2004

5 7 9 8 6

ISBN: 1 900988 909

Printed & bound by Times Offset (M) Sdn.Bhd.

British Library Catalogue in Publication Data:
A catalogue record for this book is available from
the British Library.

Introduction

Etiquette is important in Arabia. Indeed, you must know something about it if you wish to get on with Arabs. But it takes time to pick up - time you may not have. In *Simple Etiquette in Arabia* I have tried to extract the key common denominators of etiquette pertaining to this large area but with a particular eye on those countries which could broadly be termed 'the Gulf region'. For the Westerner this is undoubtedly one of the most active areas in the whole of Arabia.

It is a well known fact that the smallest efforts of the foreigner in learning Arabic can earn a disproportionate amount of kudos and appreciation. Speaking Arabic need not be difficult – even for those who claim to be bad at languages. *Very Simple Arabic* is a highly selective phrase-book and elementary language guide. The few vital phrases needed in the most commonly experienced situations can be quickly found. For those who wish to go further I have also included a simple explanation of grammar and a vocabulary of useful words.

JAMES PETERS

Acknowledgements

The publishers and I wish to express our thanks to those who have given advice in the making of this book. For *Simple Etiquette in Arabia*, we are especially grateful to Hussein Dabbagh, Frederick Sullivan, Paul Mahmood and Dr S. Darsh, former Imam of the London Mosque. For *Very Simple Arabic*, we are indebted to Patrick de Courcy-Ireland and the late Desmond Cosgrove. Finally, for their help with the fully revised combined edition, we express our thanks to Richard Palmer and Daoud and Leila Dallal.

J.P.

PART I

Simple Etiquette
in
ARABIA

Contents

A Note on Pronunciation

Arabic words (*written in italics)* are intended to be pronounced as the English spelling suggests, except that:

aa	is pronounced as	'a' in 'father'	
ow	"	"	'ow' in 'how'
u	"	"	'u' in 'put'
dh	"	"	'th' in 'the'
kh	"	"	'ch' in 'loch'
gh	"	"	'r' in French 'rue'
ei	"	"	'eye'
q	"	"	a guttural 'k'
'	"	"	a glottal stop

There are no capital letters in Arabic, where necessary the stress syllable is shown in bold type and doubled consonants should be given extra stress. Finally, the definite article *'al'* is linked to its noun or adjective by a hyphen.

Although most beginners are naturally shy about pronouncing words which are strange to them, do not be put off. Arabs are used to hearing a variety of accents from within the Arab world and will generally be delighted that you have made the effort. Do not take correction as criticism - it will improve your fluency and establish a rapport.

1

Some Useful Facts

Most Arabs are Muslims (it is also spelt Moslem). Their religion, Islam, revealed by God to the Prophet Muhammad between 610 and 632 AD plays a vital role in their lives.

This revelation is recorded in the Holy Quran, and is considered by Muslims to be the infallible word of God. It contains among other things a comprehensive code of conduct governing every aspect of a believer's life.

The public place of worship is the Mosque …

... which is attended mainly by men. Women either pray at home or use the special place allotted in most large Mosques. The call to prayer is chanted by the Muezzin from the Minaret ...

On entering the Mosque and before praying the Muslim removes his shoes and washes his hands, face and feet. Prayer is led by the Imam.

Friday is the holy day of the week, although a Muslim must pray five times every day at:

Dawn
Noon
Afternoon
Sunset
Evening

Daily prayers do not have to be said in a Mosque. Muslims pray wherever they happen to be at the time of prayer. This may be in an office or beside a road; don't be surprised, therefore, when you first see it. In Arabia it is a common everyday sight.

A Muslim, when he prays, always faces in the direction of the Holy City of Makkah.

Arabic is the language of the Holy Quran. The rudiments of the spoken language can be quickly mastered once you get down to it and the script, written from right to left, although it looks complicated, is not that difficult to learn when simply explained.*

The pleasantries are included in subsequent chapters and if a foreigner takes the trouble to learn them he can be sure of an enthusiastic reception. In the author's experience, one is invariably given greater credit than is justified by one's efforts.

* See *Very Simple Arabic Script* - James Peters 2003

4

Women in many Arab countries wear a black cloak and head scarf and may also wear a mask (*hijaab*). In other Arab countries however, women dress in the Western fashion. In either case, women are viewed in a special way in Arabia. One might, for example, enquire after the health of the family of an Arab but not specifically of his wife.

The thing most likely to impress you about the Arab is his hospitality …

bay*tee* **bay***tak*

My house is your house

…but his whole way of life, stemming as it does from his ancient heritage as well as from his environment, may well catch your imagination.

2

On Meeting An Arab

Always shake hands. When they greet each other it is customary for Arabs who are close friends to kiss symbolically on each cheek. An Arab may also keep hold of your hand while he is talking to you after shaking hands. This is a normal custom in Arabia and is a mark of friendship.

The most common greetings are as follows:

General Greeting (at any time)

as-salaam alaykum

Greeting

wa alaykum as-salaam

Reply

Welcome

ahlan wa sahlan

Greeting

ahlan wa sahlan beek*

Reply

* *beekum* if replying to more than one person and *beekee* if replying to a woman

Good Morning

Greeting

Reply

Good Afternoon
or
Good Evening

Greeting

Reply

How are you?

*kayf **haa**lak**

*al-**ham**doolillah bi-**khair***

Greeting   Reply

* *kayf **haa**lik?* to a woman. The reply is the same.

The reply *al-**ham**doolillah bi-**khair*** or simply *al-**ham**doolillah* on its own, means that you are well (lit. 'Thanks be to God - I am well') and it is customary always to give this reply even if you are at death's door. In saying this the Muslim is acknowledging God's will over all things.

Hello

murahuba*   murahuba

Greeting   Reply

orms of address are important. An Arab is called '*sayed*' (Mr) followed by his given and family names, and when on familiar terms by the first of his given names only. A ruling Shaikh** is 'Your Highness' initially and thereafter 'Sir'. Other Shaikhs are 'Your Excellency' as are Government Ministers. When calling an Arab it is polite to prefix his name with '*ya*' …

ya ahmed!

* Less formal greeting used in some Arab countries strictly meaning 'Welcome!' Exceptionally the *u* in *murahuba* is pronounced as the *u* in 'but'.
** Pronounced as in Eng. 'shake' and not as in 'chic'.

The two main variations for 'Goodbye' are:

and

You may also hear **allah yisullmak** and **salaamakallah** used in reply.

3
You Pay A Call

After shaking hands and exchanging greetings the person on whom you call will ask you to sit down…

Your host will indicate a seat. The most important visitor usually sits on his host's right hand in the closest seat.

Don't be surprised if someone occupying that position gets up to make way for you. It means you are considered more important ...for the moment anyway.

Don't sit in such a way that the sole of your foot is presented to another person. This used to mean, and still does in some places, that you are intentionally insulting that person (since the sole of the foot is unclean).

What happens next depends on your host. He may or may not follow the custom of consuming refreshments before discussing the purpose of your visit. His manner and general appearance will usually tell you what type of person he is. It is increasingly common in business circles to dispense with some of the formalities.

If however, your host abides by the old customs there can then follow a period of silence or general enquiries after each other's health. This lasts until a servant enters with tea or coffee.

Take the coffee cup in the right hand. The right hand only is used when drinking, eating and offering anything to someone.

Drink as many cups as you like but not a lot more than your host or others present. It is customary, however, to drink more than one cup of coffee or milkless tea or you risk offending your host. Turkish coffee should be sipped until an inch of the liquid remains in the cup or you may end up swallowing the thick coffee grounds.

The signal that you use to show you have had enough to drink is a quick twist of the empty cup as you hand it back.

The time should now be opportune to mention the subject of your visit.

You may, as a businessman, have been ushered into a room and found other businessmen present. In this case, announce yourself, sit down, drink any refreshment offered and wait to be asked your business. When asked, give enough information to interest your potential client so that he will consider granting you an exclusive interview later when you will be able to talk privately.

Do not admire anything belonging to your host. By custom, he may feel obliged to make you a gift of it! Even if you succeed in refusing it may take a long time.

It is inadvisable to work to a tight schedule in Arabia. Be on time for an appointment, but be prepared for it to be delayed (you may be kept waiting for a considerable time) or even postponed. This is not inefficiency but simply the result of a different approach to life lived at a different pace. You will also find that many Arabs keep 'open office', *i.e.* other people are free to enter at any time.

If you hand a gift to an Arab friend do not be surprised if he does not open it or even thank you for it. This is the normal custom in Arabia although it is difficult for Westerners to understand. He will also frequently start to refuse the gift, indicating that you should not have taken the trouble. But you should politely insist the gift be accepted.

Remembering Arab names can be difficult but it is important to get them right. Most Arabs have printed cards in English and Arabic. It will help to have your own card printed in the same way.

finally, never call at siesta time …

4
A Hafla

The Arabic word for a party is *hafla*. You may be fortunate enough to receive an invitation. In which case …

Your host would be impressed to receive a written reply in Arabic, if that is appropriate. An Arab friend might write it for you.

The time of your arrival will vary depending on the type and circumstances of the party and who the host is. It is sometimes correct to arrive exactly on time and at others to delay for five or so minutes or even longer. It is best to seek advice …

Eating still sometimes takes place at floor level, in which case you should remove your shoes as you enter the dining room. Again, avoid presenting the soles of your feet to anyone and use only your right hand...

I t is customary to take your leave soon after you have drunk coffee at the end of the meal…

Y ou may also wish to entertain. Ideally, issue a written invitation in Arabic. Any local printer will help you. Do not attempt to mimic all the Arab customs. English food is quite acceptable except that the Muslim is forbidden by the laws of his religion to eat pork or drink alcohol.

When an Arab has visited you he may later make a small gift in thanks. You should reciprocate when next you are his guest.

5

Eeds

The Arabic word for a festival is *eed*. There are a number of important religious festivals each year but you need only concern yourself with the two main ones ...

eed al-adha   and   eed al-fitr

23

he exact date of any festival varies every year because the Muslim calendar (Hegirian) is based on the lunar cycle.

he largest festival is the *eed al-**adha*** which is celebrated at the end of the annual pilgrimage to Makkah. A major feature of the pilgrimage is the circumambulation of the **ka'ba**, the cube shaped building in the Grand Mosque in Makkah which holds the Black Stone sacred to all Muslims.

he other main festival, the *eed al-fitr*, takes place at the end of the fast of Ramadan.

Ramadan lasts for a full lunar month. All Muslims are required to abstain from food, drink and tobacco and all other pleasurable pursuits between sunrise and sunset.

Naturally you should show consideration and not eat, drink or smoke in the presence of a Muslim during daylight hours. In any case, you will probably find it is a punishable offence to do so in some Arab countries. A Western woman should, in addition, dress soberly, *i.e.* she should not wear a short skirt.

Ramadan ends with a feast.

O n the occasion of both the *eed al-adha* and the *eed al-fitr* greetings cards are sent to friends and important business clients (to arrive a day or two in advance). The cards one should send, which are available from Arab card shops and printers, look like this...

Y ou should not forget to sign the card.

Y ou will sometimes receive a card of thanks in reply. This card will look like this:

When you meet an Arab on the day of a festival or in the days closely following it you would shake hands and use a special greeting:

Greeting   Reply

* Alternatively you will hear *ayaamak saeeda*.

On the occasion of both festivals it is the custom for important persons to hold audience in their palaces or homes. You should enter the house, greet them, take coffee and leave after a suitable interval.

Arab families and friends visit each other at *eed* time and a visiting foreigner would be equally welcome during this period.

you may also give a small present to the children of an Arab family if you visit one.

ONE AT A TIME LADS!

6

Miscellaneous Points

The first problem you face in Arabia may be the heat. It can make people who are not used to it tired and perhaps short tempered.

The laws concerning alcohol and drugs are strictly enforced in some Arab countries where the possession of even a small quantity of alcohol is punishable with imprisonment and the possession of drugs a capital offence…

You may also find a ban on the 'Playboy' type of magazine. Advice on all these matters can easily be obtained from an airline or travel agent before departure.

Taxis in Arabia seldom have meters. It is wise for a newcomer to agree the fare in advance of the journey and so avoid any surprises. Tipping of taxi drivers is customary in some Arab countries but not in the Gulf region; tipping of porters is universal. Tipping in hotels and restaurants follows Western practice, *i.e.* tip if there is no service charge.

It is often difficult for a Westerner to understand that prices in an Arab market (*sooq*) are flexible. Bargaining is part of the way of life. There are of course plenty of other shops where prices are fixed but this will be obvious to you.

In general conversation with an Arab, at least on first acquaintance, avoid talking about religion, women and the politics of the Arab world.

You will discover that the Arab sense of humour is remarkably similar to our own. However, avoid telling jokes until you know someone well.

Don't be surprised when offering something to an Arab – say a drink – if he says '*shukraan*' or 'thank you' but means by that that he refuses. This is a customary way of saying 'no' in Arabia.

If you are unfortunate enough to be involved in an accident of any kind in Arabia, keep your cool whatever the rights and wrongs of the matter. It always pays to be calm, dignified and polite…

You should be aware that in Arabia a dog in considered unclean, except perhaps for the Saluki – the Arabian gazelle hound.

An Arab uses his hands as a means of expression as much as a Frenchman does. Among the examples of Arab gestures are …

… putting the tips of the fingers and thumb together and moving the hand up and down again to mean 'Patience!', 'Patience!'

… pulling the point of one's chin to mean …

… 'Shame!'

… and putting the fingers together and pointing downwards when beckoning someone …

… do not beckon with one finger in the normal way as this has an offensive connotation in Arabia.

*S*ooner or later you will come across a variation of the customary handshake. If his hands are dirty, an Arab will offer you his right wrist which you should shake in the normal way.

Great care should be taken when producing a document or advertisement in Arabic. It is easy for a translator to render an English phrase into Arabic and for the result to be meaningless or even offensive.

Finally, here are six very common words, not previously mentioned, which you may find useful:

Please

Thank you   You're welcome!

* Other words are *mashkoor* and *ashkoorak*.
** *See* Glossary on page 37.

Be pleased to …

(when offering a seat, coffee, food, etc.)

If God wills

Sorry! *(or muta'assif)*

aasif	'Sorry' (also *muta'**assif*** and ***af**wan*)
afwan	'I beg your pardon' (but in reply to 'Thank you', You're welcome!)
ahlan wa **sah**lan!	'Welcome!'
ahlan wa **sah**lan beek	Reply to **ah**lan wa **sah**lan (**bee**kum to more than one person and **bee**kee to a woman)
al-**ham**doolil**lah**!	'Thanks be to God - well!' (reply to 'How are you?')
allah yu**baar**ak feek	Reply to *eed mu**baa**rak*
allah yi**sull**mak	Reply to *ma' as-sa**laa**ma*
as-sa**laam** a**lay**kum	'Peace be upon you' (general greeting)
a**yaa**mak sa**eed**a!	'May your days be happy' (alt.reply to *eed mu**baa**rak*!)
bak**sheesh**!	'A tip!' (begging)
baytee **bay**tak	'My house is your house'
eed	Festival
eed al-**adh**a	Festival at the end of the Pilgrimage
eed al-fitr	Festival at the end of the fast of Ramadan
eed mu**baa**rak!	Greeting at *eed* time. (*lit.* 'Congratulations on the *eed*!')

37

fee amaan allah	'Goodbye' (also *ma' as-salaama*)
hijaab	A mask worn by some Arab women.
ka'ba	Cube-shaped building in the Grand Mosque in Makkah holding the sacred Black Stone.
kayf haalak?	'How are you?' (to a man)
layf haalik?	'How are you?' (to a woman)
hafla	A party
imam	Leader of prayers in a mosque (*imaam*)
insha'alah	'If God wills' (common reply acknowledging God's will over all things)
mashkoor	'Thank you'
masaa' al-khair	'Good afternoon/evening'
masaa' an-noor	Reply to *masaa' al-khair*
ma' as-salaama	'Goodbye' (*lit.* 'With the peace'
murahuba	'Hello/welcome!' The *u* is pronounced as in 'but')
muta'assif	'Sorry' (also *aasif* and *afwan*)
Minaret	Mosque tower (*manaara/ mi'dhana*)
minfadlak	'Please' (*minfadlik* to a woman)
Muezzin	Caller to prayer (*mu'adhin*)
Ramadan	the month of the fast (*ramadhaan*)
sabaah al-khair	'Good morning'
sabaah an-noor	Reply to 'Good morning'
salaamakallah	Reply to *ma' as-salaama* (lit. 'In the peace of God')
shukraan	'Thank you'
sooq	Market
tafaddal	Please sit down/please accept something (lit. 'Be pleased to...')
wa alaykum as-salaam	Reply to *as-salaam alaykum*
ya ahmed	Polite form of address (lit. 'Oh Ahmed')

PART II

Very Simple
ARABIC

Contents

On Arrival
General Greeting

as-salaam alaykum
(Greeting)
Peace be with you

wa alaykum as-salaam
(Reply)
And with you peace

Welcome

ahlan wa sahlan!
(Greeting)

ahlan wa sahlan beek*
(Reply)

* *beekum* to more than one person, *beekee* to a woman.

Good Morning

sabaah al-*khair*	*sabaah* an-*noor*
(Greeting)	(Reply)

Good Afternoon

and

Good Evening

masaa' al-*khair*	*masaa'* an-*noor*
(Greeting)	(Reply)

How are you?

*kayf **haa**lak? ** *   *al-**ham**doolil**lah** bi-**khair***

(Greeting)   (Reply)

How are you?*   Thanks be to God (I am well)

* *kayf **haa**lik*? To a woman. The reply is the same.

and you?

wa inta?   *al-**ham**doolil**lah***

(Greeting)   (Reply)

Goodbye

*ma' as-sal**aam**a*	*allah yisallmak*
(Greeting)	(Reply)
(Go) with the peace	God give you peace

Good Night

tisbah ala khair	*wa inta min **ah**lah*
(Greeting)	(Reply)
Rise well	And you

See you tomorrow

*ashoofak **buk**ra*

Hello

*mura**huba****

(Greeting)

*mura**huba***

(Reply)

* Less formal greeting used in some Arab countries strictly meaning ''Welcome!''. Exceptionally the *u* in *mura**huba*** is pronounced as the *u* in 'but'. Alternative replies include *murahuba**tayn*** and ***ah**lan*!

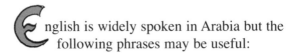

nglish is widely spoken in Arabia but the following phrases may be useful:

What is your name?	*aysh ismak?*
My name is John Smith	*ismee john smith*
Do you speak English?	*tatakallum ingleezee?*
I don't understand	*ma afham*
I have only this (to declare)	*eindee haadha faqat**
I have nothing (to declare)	*ma eindee shee*
This is necessary for my work (e.g. samples)	*haadha dharooree li-amalee*
Porter!	*hammaal!*
That is mine	*haadhihi lee*
Where is my bag?	*wayn shantatee?*
There is one bag missing	*naaqas shanta*
Where is the toilet please?	*wayn al-hammaam minfadlak?*
Get me a taxi please	*utlub lee taaksee minfadlak*
How much (is that)?	*kam?*
How many kilometres is it to the town?	*kam keeloomitr lil-balad?*
I want to hire a car	*ureed astaa'jir seiyaara*
Where is the bus to the city?	*wayn al-baas lil-madeena?*
Where is the British Consulate?	*wayn al-consuleeya al-bareetaaneeya?*

* You will also hear '*bass*'- the alternative word for 'only'

2

In A Taxi

*ilal-**fun**duk shira**toon** min**fad**lak*

To the Sheraton Hotel please

*ei**wa** (or na'am) **see**dee*

Yes, Sir

kam?

How much?

khamsta'shar deenaar

Fifteen Dinars

la, katheer

No, (that is) a lot

itna'shar deenaar

Twelve Dinars

teiyyib!

Good!

kam keeloomitr ilal-heeltoon?

How many kilometres to the Hilton?

ashara, seedee

Ten, Sir

If you wish to give directions

ruh seeda, minfadlak

Go straight ahead, please

*ilal-ya**saar** hina*

To the left here

*ilal-ya**meen**!*

To the right!

*wo**qq**of hinaak min**fad**lak*

Stop there please

*bi-**sur**'a min**fad**lak*

Faster please

*bi-**but'** min**fad**lak*

Slower please

intadhar hina minfadlak

Wait here please

aarja' ba' ad khamsa daqaa'iq

I will be back in five minutes

3
In An Hotel

*as-sa**laam** a**lay**kum*

(Greeting)

Peace be with you

*wa a**lay**kum as-sa**laam***

(Reply)

And with you peace

*is**mee** bee**ters****

My name is Peters

* There is no 'p' or 'v' in Arabic and 'b' and 'f' are
  substituted respectively.

*ein*dee *hajz*

I have a reservation

*ureed ghur*fa *min**fad**lak*

I want a room please

*ureed ghur*fa *li-shakh**sain** laha ham**maam***

I want a double room with a bath

*fee mu**kay**yif?*

Is there air conditioning?

*kam al-ee**jaar** li-**mud**dat yome?*

How much is it (lit. 'the rent') per day?

***ein**dak **ghur**fa **ar**khas min **dhaa**lik?*

Have you a room cheaper than that?

ureed ashoof al-ghurfa minfadlak

I want to see the room please

la ma-ahibha

No. I don't like it

fee ghurfa ahsan?

Is there a better room?

haadha teiyyib

This is fine

meen?

Who?

risaala, seedee

A message, Sir

lahdha minfadlak

A moment please

ta'aal!

Come in!

illak, seedee

For you, Sir

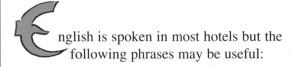

nglish is spoken in most hotels but the following phrases may be useful:

What is the number of my room?	*aysh raqm **ghur**fatee?*
My room number is …	*raqm **ghur**fatee …*
This is broken	***haa**dha mak**soor***
This is my laundry	***haa**dha gha**seelee***
When will it be ready?	***aym**ta **haa**dhir?*
I want to leave this in the safe	*u**reed** a**trak haa**dha fil-**khaz**na*
Is there a message for Mr Peters?	*fee ri**saa**la lis-**sei**yid **beet**ers?*
Where is the telephone please?	*wayn at-tili**foon**/al-**haa**tif min**fad**lak?*
I want telephone number...	*u**reed** raqm at-tili**foon**/al-**haa**tif …*
I want to send a fax	*u**reed** ar**sil** fax*
I want to post a letter	*u**reed** ar**sil** mak**toob** bil-bar**eed***
Have you got an English newspaper?	*ein**dak** ja**ree**da inglee**zee**ya?*
I want to change some travellers' cheques	*u**reed** tah**weel** shee**kaat** seeyaa**hee**ya*
I want a taxi please	*u**reed** taxi min**fad**lak*
I want to hire a car with a driver/without a driver	*u**reed** as**taa'**jir sei**yaa**ra bi-**saa'**iq/bi**doon saa'**iq*
I am in a hurry	*ana mus**ta'**jil*
The bill please	*al-hi**saab** min**fad**lak*
What is this?	*aysh **haa**dha?*
There is a mistake here	*fee **gha**lat hina*

4

Calling On An Arab

When calling on an Arab, as well as knowing the basic rules of etiquette, a knowledge of the phrases below will give an excellent impression.

Welcome!

*ah*lan wa *sah*lan!   *ah*lan wa *sah*lan beek*

(Greeting)   (Reply)

* *bee*kum if replying to more than one person and *bee*kee to a woman.

*kayf **haa**lak?** *al-**ham**doolil**lah** bi-**khair***

(Greeting) (Reply)

How are you? Thanks be to God
  - I am well

* *kayf **haa**lik?* To a woman. The reply is the same.

*min**fad**lak astar**reeh*** *mash**koor****

Please have a seat Thank you

* Variant of *shuk**raan*** and *ash**koor**ak*.

*ta**fad**dal **qah**wa?*   *ei**wa* or ***na**'am*

Please have coffee?   Yes*

*ta**fad**dal***

Have this

*shuk**raan**, bi**kaf**fee*

Thank you, (*i.e.* 'no') I have had sufficient

---

* It would be impolite to refuse. Do not say *shuk**raan***
  (thank you) as in Arabia, in this context, it means 'no'.

** Lit. 'be pleased to'.

***bay**tee **bay**tak*

My house is your house

*shar**raft**na*

lit. 'You have honoured me/us'– said by the host

*shukran ja**zee**lan*   *ma'-as-sa**laam**a*

Thank you very much   Goodbye

5
Shopping

kam?	*ih*da'shar *deen*aar
How much?	Eleven Dinars

*shuk**raan***, a'**teek kham**sa*   *tha**maan**ia, **see**dee*

Thank you, (*i.e.* 'no'*)   Eight, Sir
I'll give you five

*tei**yyib**, laakin **ghaa**lee*   *la, ra**khees***
Good, but (it is) expensive   No, it is cheap

---

* 'Thank you' meaning 'no' - *see* page 61

haadha ad-dukkaan maftooh?

Is this shop open?

la, musakkar

No, it is closed

tureed shee seedee?

You want something, Sir?

la, atafarraj faqat

No, I'm only looking round

*shoof **see**dee, shoof!*

Look Sir, Look!

*shuk**raan**, la!*

Thank you, No!

In case you are troubled ....

*bak**sheesh**! bak**sheesh**!* **im**shee!*

Baksheesh! Baksheesh!   Go!

* A tip! A tip!

*wayn **mak**tab al-ba**reed** min**fad**lak?*

hinaak …

Where is the post office please?

There …

he words below may be substituted in this sentence…

Antique Shop	*duk**kaan** antee**qaat***
Bank	*bank*
Bazaar	*sooq*
Bookshop/stationer	***mak**taba*
Chemist	*seidal**lee**ya*
Clothes Shop	*duk**kaan** ma**laa**bis*
Dry Cleaner	*duk**kaan** tand**theef** ma**laa**bis*
Florist	*duk**kaan** zu**hoor***
Jeweller	*jow**aah**irjee*
Newsagent	***baa**'i jaraa'id*
Perfumery	*al-'aa**taar***
Photographic Shop	*duk**kaan** tas**weer**/i**stud**iyoo*
Shoe Shop	*duk**kaan** ah**dhee**ya*
Sports Shop	*duk**kaan** reeyaa**dee**ya*
Stationer/Bookshop	***mak**taba*
Tailor	*khay**yaat***
Tobacconist	*duk**kaan** sa**gaa**yer*
Travel Agent	*wa**kaa**lat safar*

ureed ishteree 'qomees'   *ta'aal!*
minfadlak

I want to buy a 'shirt' please   Come!

The words below may be substituted in this sentence …

Book	*kitaab*
Cigarettes	*sagaayer*
Dictionary	*qaamoos*
Envelopes	*dhuroof*
Film	*film*
Guide book	*kitaab daleel*
Hat	*qubba'a*
Map of the town	*khaaritat al-balad*
Magazine	*majalla*
Newspaper	*jareeda*
Notebook	*daftar*
Paper Tissues	*mandeel woroq*
Pen	*qolum hibr*
Pencil	*qolum rusaas*
Razor Blades	*moos hallaaqa*
Tobacco	*tombaaq*
Toothbrush	*fursha lil-asnaan*
Toothpaste	*ma'joon lil-asnaan*
Towel	*manshafa*
Writing Paper	*woroq al-kitaaba*

6
Travelling Around and Sightseeing

as-salaam alaykum
(Greeting)

wa daykum as-salaam
(Reply)

Peace be with you

And with you peace

wayn mahattat al-baas minfadlak?

Where is the bus station please?

awwal sharri'a alal-yasaar

The first street on the left

*ba'**eed** min hina?*

Far from here?

      *la, q**oreeb**, **kham**sa da**qaa**'iq faqat*

      No, it is close, five minutes only

mumkin **maa**shee?

Is it possible to walk?

      *ei**wa**, **arb**a'a **mi**'at mitr*

      Yes, four hundred metres

*u**reed** al-baas ila as-sooq min**fad**lak*

I want the bus to the sooq please.

*haa**dhaak***

That one

*ila as-sooq min**fad**lak*

To the sooq please

*ta**fad**dal*

Be pleased to (get in)

aymta tarooh?

When do you go?

ba'ad ashara daqaa'iq

After ten minutes

khabirnee eind al-wusool minfadlak

Inform me when we arrive please

eiwa
Yes

*u**reed** a**zoor** al-mat'**haf** minfadlak*

I want to visit the Museum please

hinaak

Over there

*fee shee mu**himm** hina?*

Is there anything of importance here?

*ei**wa**, ta'**aal***

Yes, come

*taxi! wayn **mak**tab as-seeyaaha'?*

Taxi! Where is the
Tourist Office? *

he following words may be substituted in the
above sentence …

The Castle	*al-**qal**'a*
The Church	*al-ka**nees**a*
The Exhibition	*al-**ma**'rid*
The Park/Gardens	*al-bus**taan***
The Library	*al-**mak**taba*
The Mosque	*al-**mas**jid*
The Old City	*al-ma**deen**a al-qo**deem**a*
The Ancient Ruins	*al-aa**thaar***
The University	*al-**jaam**i'a*
The Zoological Gardens	*al-ha**deeq**at al-heiyawaa**naat***

* Lit. (the) office (of) the tourism. See the explanation of
'Possession' on pages 102 and 103.

7
Leisure

A Pavement Café

*lay**moon baar**id min**fad**lak*

A cold lemon drink please

*kam tu**reed**?*

How many do you want?

*ith**nayn** min**fad**lak*

Two please

*fee **mat**'am **qoreeb** min hina?*

Is there a restaurant near here?

minfadlak, nureed kabaab

Please, we would like a kebab

The following words may be substituted in this sentence…

Beer	*beera* *	Oranges	*burtuqaal*
Boiled	*maslooq*	Pepper	*filfil*
Bread	*khubz*	Potatoes	*bataata*
Butter	*zibda*	Rice	*ruz*
Cheese	*jubna*	Salad	*salaata*
Chicken	*dajaaj*	Salt	*milh*
Coffee	*qahwa*	Sandwich	*sandweesh*
Eggs	*baydh*	Sauce/Gravy	*salsa*
Fish	*samak*	Soup	*shoorba*
Fried/Roasted	*maqlee*	Sugar	*sukkarr*
Fruit	*fawaakih*	Tea	*shei*
Lemon	*laymoon*	Tomatoes	*tamaata*
Meat	*lahm*	Vegetables	*khudhra*
Melon	*botteekh*	Water	*moya/ma'*
Milk	*haleeb*	Wine	*nbeedh* *

* In those countries where drinking alcohol is permitted.

*ein*dak *qah*wa *nes*cafay?

Have you got Nescafé?

*la, tur**keeya** bass*

No, Turkish coffee only

*al-hi**saab** min**fad**lak*

The bill please

***ureed** a**zoor** **maq**ha minfadlak*

I want to visit a coffee-house please

The following words may be substituted:

cinema	***seen**amaa*
night club	***malha** **layli***
theatre	***mas**rah*

fee ***cab**aaray?*

Is there a floor show?

The following words may be substituted:

belly-dancer	***raa**qisa shar**qee**ya*
music	***moo**seeqa*
dancing	*raqs*

***mum**kin **al**'ab **ten**nees hina?*

Is it possible to play tennis here?

he following words may be substituted in this sentence:

golf   *goolf*
bowling   ***boo**ling*

*fee **mas**bah hina?*   *ma'**loom**!*

Is there a swimming   Of course,
pool here?   certainly!

ureed asbah fil-bahr minfadlak

I want to swim in the sea please

fee khatar hina?

Is there any danger here?

mumkin sayd as-samak hina?

Is it possible to fish here?

8

Some Useful Expressions

*muta'**assif**! (or **aas**if!)*

Sorry!

*ana ma fa**himt***   I didn't understand

*is**mah**lee*   Excuse me

maa laysh (or *maa yu**khaa**lif*)   Never mind

(Often accompanied by a shrug of the shoulders)

shukraan   *la shukra ala-waajib!* *

Thank you   Don't mention it!

    * Lit. 'Don't thank me, it is my duty'.

inta loteef

You are kind

*inta ameri**kaan**ee/in**gleez**ee?*

Are you American/English?

*la, ana in**gleez**ee/ameri**kaan**ee*

No, I am English/American

*tata**kullum** **arab**ee? bass qoleel*

Do you speak Arabic? Only a little

Congratulations

*ma**brook**!*

Lit. 'Blessed'

*allah yu**baar**ak feek*

Lit. 'God bless you (too)'

At Festival Time

*eed mu**baar**ak!* *

(Greeting)

*allah yu**baar**ak feek*

(Reply)

* Words used at the time of the two main religious festivals – *see* Part I: Simple Etiquette in Arabia

Exclamations!

*ya sa**laam**!*

Good Lord!

__wal__lah!

By God!

mumtaaz!

Excellent!

al-hamdoolillah!

Thanks be to God!

89

*ashoofak **buk**ra*   *i**sha**'alah!* *

See you tomorrow   If God wills!

* A common reply acknowledging God's will over all
things. lit. If (it is) the will of God.

*fee hal**laaq** hina min**fad**lak?*

Is there a barber here please?

*wayn fee to**beeb** min**fad**lak?*

Where is there a doctor please?

he following can be subsituted in this sentence…

dentist	*to**beeb** al-as**naan***
optician	*ikh**saa'ee** an-nadha**raat***

***ein**dee **waja**' hina*

I have a pain here

*haadha mak**soor***

This (is) broken

nd finally:

*aysh ism **haa**dha, min**fad**lak?*

What do you call this, please?

*aysh **ma'**ana **haa**dha?*

What does this mean?

*kul-lee marra **thaan**eeya min**fad**lak*

Tell me again please

***ut**lub to**beeb**/ sei**yaara** al-is'**aaf** - bi-**sur'a**!*

Call a doctor/ambulance - quickly!

***ut**lub ash-**shur**ta!*

Call the Police!

9
Numbers
and
Days of the Week

0	٠	*sifr*
1	١	**waa**hid
2	٢	ith**nayn**
3	tha**laatha**
4	٤	**arb**a'a
5	٥	**khams**a
6	٦	sit**ta**
7	٧	**saba**'a
8	٨	tha**maan**ia
9	٩	**tis**'a
10	١٠	**ash**ara

N.B. The Arabic zero should not be confused with our
decimal point (normally a comma in Arabic) or the
Arabic 'five' with our zero.

11	١١	*hida'shar*
12	١٢	*itna'shar*
13	١٣	*thalaathta'shar*
14	١٤	*arba'ata'shar*
15	١٥	*khamsta'shar*
16	١٦	*sitt'ashar*
17	١٧	*saba'ata'shar*
18	١٨	*thamaanta'shar*
19	١٩	*tisa'ta'shar*
20	٢٠	*ishreen*
30	٣٠	*thalaatheen*
40	٤٠	*arba'een*
50	٥٠	*khamseen*
60	٦٠	*sitteen*
70	٧٠	*saba'een*
80	٨٠	*thamaanee-een*
90	٩٠	*tisa'een*
100	١٠٠	*meeya*
1,000	١٠٠٠	*elf* (pl. *alaaf*)
1,000,000	١٬٠٠٠٬٠٠٠	*milyoon*

Numbers after twenty are made up as follows:

$$25 = \textbf{\textit{kham}}\textit{sa wa ish}\textbf{\textit{reen}}$$
$$26 = \textit{sitta wa ish}\textbf{\textit{reen}}$$

There is no indefinite article (a/an) in Arabic and it is unnecessary to qualify a single object by using **waa**hid (one) e.g. *walad* means 'a' or 'one' boy.

There is a special way of saying two of anything in Arabic. You add the ending '*ayn*' to the noun:

walad   *walad***ayn**

This form of plural is called the 'dual'.

*f*rom 3 to 10 the accompanying noun is in the plural *but* from eleven onwards it is in the singular, *e.g*
.

> *tha**laatha** awlaad* = three boys
> *ish**reen** walad* = twenty boys

*C*omposite numbers are written from left to right, *e.g.*

٢٠٠٤ = 2004

(Unlike the Arabic script which is written from right to left)

Days of the Week

Sunday	*yome al-**ah**ad*
Monday	*yome al-ith**nayn***
Tuesday	*yome ath-tha**laatha***
Wednesday	*yome al-**arba**'a*
Thursday	*yome al-kha**mees***
Friday	*yome al-**juma**'a*
Saturday	*yome as-sabt*

CHAPTER 10 - SIMPLE GRAMMAR

Although the Arabic script appears daunting it is not as complicated as it looks.* There are only a few more letters and sounds than in English and the rules of grammar are, if anything, more logical.

The script runs from right to left but composite numbers are written from left to right.

In common with other Semitic languages, a major feature of Arabic is that most words are based on a three-letter verbal root.

For example the three letters *k t b* of the verb *katab* (he wrote) are the root concerned with writing and from it derive *kitaab* (a book), *kaatib* (a clerk), *maktab* (an office), *maktaba* (a library) and other verbs such as *kaatab* (to correspond with).

There is no indefinite article 'a' in Arabic and:

walad means 'a boy'

The definite article 'the' is '*al*' and is attached to the word it qualifies. In front of words beginning with *t th d dh s sh r z n* and sometimes *g*, the '*l*' of the article is assimilated *e.g. al-shams* (the sun) becomes *ash-shams*.

The gender of nouns is either masculine or feminine. Nouns referring only to females are obviously feminine and so too are most nouns ending in '*a*'. But otherwise there is often no clue as to the correct gender, which must be learned.

As explained in Chapter 9, there are three 'numbers' in Arabic - singular, dual and plural.

* See *Very Simple Arabic Script*. James Peters 2003

Plurals are not formed as in English. They are mostly variants of the singular and again are best memorised. However, masculine nouns referring to people form their plural simply by adding '*een*' e.g.

Singular ***muslim*** (m)   Plural *musli**meen***

and feminine nouns ending in '*a*' form their plural by adding '*aat*' e.g. 'a government':

Singular *hukooma* (f)   Plural *hukoo**maat***

Adjectives follow the noun and if the noun is definite then the adjective also carries the definite article *e.g.*

*al-walad as-sa**gheer*** = The small boy

Normally they agree with the noun in gender and number. However, when the noun refers to plural 'things' or 'animals' then the adjective is put in the feminine singular by adding the suffix '*a*' *e.g.*

*as-sana**waat** al-a**kheera*** = The recent years

The comparative of most adjectives take the form:

***ak**bar*	greater
***ar**khas*	cheaper
***ak**thar*	more

There is no infinitive form of the verb in Arabic (e.g. 'to write') and the third person singular (*i.e.* *katab* 'he wrote') is used instead. Verbs are conjugated in only two tenses - one denoting complete action and the other, incomplete action. In simple terms this means a past tense and a present/future tense.

For example:

katab means	he wrote (past)
yaktub means	he is writing (present)
or	he will write (future)

However, to leave no doubt that the future tense is intended the prefixes '*sa*' or '*ba*' are used *e.g.*

     sa-**yak**tub   he will write

The past tense of the simple regular verb is formed by attaching suffixes to the basic root:

kata**bt**	I wrote
kata**bt**	you (masc) wrote
katab**tee**	you (fem) wrote
katab	he wrote
kata**bat**	she wrote
katab**na**	we wrote
katab**too**	you (pl) wrote
katab**oo**	they wrote

The present/future tense is formed by adding a prefix (and sometimes a suffix as well) to the modified root and changing the second vowel:

aktub	I write/will write
taktub	you (masc) write/will write
taktu**bee**	you (fem) write/will write
yaktub	he writes/will write
taktub	she writes/will write
naktub	we write/will write
taktu**boo**	you (pl) write/will write
yaktu**boo**	they write/will write

The vowel change varies and must be learnt for each verb.

Note that the subject pronoun (I, you, he etc.) is normally omitted when using a verb in Arabic. *e.g.*

> *katab ki**taab*** means 'he wrote a book'

The 'imperative' is formed on the pattern:

> ***uk**tub*! = Write!

In spoken Arabic a negative is expressed by putting '*maa*' in front of the verb:

> *maa ka**tabt*** = I did not write
> *maa **ak**tub* = I am not writing

The imperative is negated by using the prefix '*laa*':

> *laa **uk**tub!* = Don't write!

A peculiarity of Arabic is that there is no verb 'to be' in the present tense. It does not exist, and:

> *al-walad sa**gheer*** means 'The boy (is) small'

In the past tense the verb 'to be' is irregular:

kunt	I was
kunt	you (masc) were
kuntee	you (fem) were
kaan	he was
***kaan**at*	she was
***kunn**aa*	we were
***kun**too*	you (masc. pl.) were
***kaan**oo*	they (masc. pl.) were

The future tense of 'to be' is also irregular:

akoon	I will be
takoon	you (masc.) will be
takoonee	you (fem.) will be
yakoon	he will be
takoon	she will be
nakoon	we will be
takoonoo	you (pl) will be
yakoonoo	they (masc. pl.) will be

'is/are there?' and 'there is/are' are translated by using '*fee*' with the noun *e.g.*

fee hallaaq hina? Is there a barber here?

fee booyoot hinnaak. There are houses there.

'there was' and 'there were' are both translated as '*kaan fee*'.

The personal pronouns are as follows:

ana	I
inta	you (masc)
intee	you (fem)
hoowa	he/it
heeya	she/it
nihna	we
intum	you (pl)
hum	they

Possession is denoted by attaching suffixes to the noun:

... *ee*	my
... *ak*	your (masc)
... *ik*	your (fem)
... *oh*	his
... *ha*	her
... *na*	our
... *kum*	your (pl)
... *hum*	their

e.g. **bay**tak = your house

When a noun has the feminine ending *'a'* then a *'t'* is put in front of the suffix. *e.g.*

seiyaaratee = my car

The object of a verb is denoted by using the same suffixes with the exception that *'ee'* becomes *'nee'*:

darabnee = he struck me

'To have' is expressed by adding the same suffixes to the word *'eind'*. *e.g.*

eindee = I have
eindak = You have

There is a special way of expressing possession between two nouns in Arabic which is known as the 'Construct State'. With this 'the boy's house' would be translated as:

bayt al-walad = (the) house (of) the boy

i.e. the definite article is dropped from the first word and 'of ' is understood.

However, names are considered to be definite and do not carry the definite article. Therefore 'Mohammed's house' would be translated as:

*bayt mu**ham**med*

In asking a question one either uses the same intonation of voice as in English or the word '*hal*' is put at the beginning of the sentence:

*ein**dak qah**wa?* = You have coffee?

*hal al-bayt ka**beer*** = Is the house big?

There is much more to Arabic Grammar than this but it is hoped that this simplified explanation will be a helpful introduction.

103

BASIC VOCABULARY

Plurals are shown in brackets
For numbers and days of the week see Chapter 9 on page 93

about	*howl*	bad	*battaal*
above	*foqe*	bag (paper)	*kees*
Abu Dhabi	*aboo dhabee*	bag (suitcase)	*shanta*
accident	*haadith*	Baghdad	*baghdaad*
	(hawaadith)	Bahrain	*al-bahrayn*
across	*aber*	baker	*khabbaaz*
adviser	*mustashaar*	bananas	*mowz*
	(mustashaareen)	bank	*bank*
after	*ba'ad*	barber	*hallaaq*
afternoon	*ba'ad adh-dhuhr*	Basra	*al-basra*
again	*marra thaaneeya*	bazaar	*sooq*
against/anti	*did*	bathroom	*hammaam*
agency	*wikaala*	beautiful	*jameel*
air conditioner	*mukayyif*	because	*leeyan*
aircraft	*teiyaara*	bed	*firaash*
	(teiyaaraat)	beer	*beera*
air force	*sillah al-jow*	before	*qobl*
airport	*mataar*	behind	*wora*
Algeria/Algiers	*al-jazaa'ir*	Beirut	*bayroot*
all	*kull*	belly	*raaqisa*
also	*eidan*	dancer	*sharqeeya*
always	*deiman*	beneath	*taht*
ambassador	*safeer (sufaraa')*	Benghazi	*benghaazee*
ambulance	*seiyaara al-is'aaf*	beside	*jamb*
America	*amreeka*	better	*ahsan*
Amman	*ammaan*	between	*bayn*
and	*wa*	big	*kabeer*
angry	*za'laan*	bill	*hisaab*
animal	*heiyawaan*	bird	*tayr (tuyoor)*
	(heiyawaanaat)	black	*aswad*
answer	*jawaab*	blue	*azraq*
anti/against	*did*	boat	*markab*
antiques	*anteeqaat*		*(maraakib)*
apples	*tuffah*	boiled	*maslooq*
April	*neesaan*	book	*kitaab (kutub)*
Arab	*arabee (arab)*	bookshop	*maktaba*
Arab Gulf (The)	*al-khaleej*	bowling	*booling*
	al-arabee	box	*sundook*
Arab League	*al-jaami'a*		*(sanaadeek)*
(The)	*al-arabeeya*	boy	*walad (awlaad)*
Arabic	*arabee*	brass	*nuhaas*
Arabic	*al-logha*	bread	*khubz*
language (the)	*al-arabeeya*	breakfast	*futoor*
army	*jeysh (juyoosh)*	bring me	*jeeblee*
assistant/		Britain	*bareetaaneeya*
deputy	*mu'aawin/*	British	*bareetaanee*
	wokeel	broken	*maksoor*
at	*eind*	brother	*akh (ikhwa)*
attack	*hujoom*	brown	*asmar*
August	*aab*	brush	*fursha (furash)*
back	*dhahr*	bus	*baas (basaat)*

bus stop	*mahattat al-baas*	contract	*aqd (uqood)*
businessman	*rajul a'maal*	cook	*tabbakh*
but	*walaakin*	correct	*soheeh*
butter	*zibda*	cost	*qeema*
he bought	*ishtaraa*	country	*bilaad (buldaan)*
he buys	*yashtaree*	crime	*jareema*
by...	*bi-*		*(jaraa'im)*
by car	*bi-seiyaara*	cross	*soleeb*
		crowd	*jumhoor*
cake	*kaa'k*		*(jamaahir)*
Cairo	*al-qaahira*	cup	*finjaan*
camel	*jamal (jimaal)*		*(fanaajeen)*
camera	*aalat at-tasweer*	custom	*'aada ('aadaat)*
car	*seiyaara*	customs	*al-jumruk*
	(seiyaaraat)	(at airport)	
carpet	*sajjaada*		
he carried	*hamal*	Damascus	*dimashq*
he carries	*yahmil*	dancing	*raqs*
castle	*qal'a*	danger	*khatar*
centre	*markaz*	date	*taareekh*
certificate	*shahaada*	date (edible)	*tamr (tumoor)*
chair	*kursee*	daughter	*bint (banaat)*
	(karaasee)	dawn	*fajr*
cheap	*rakhees*	day	*yome (ayaam)*
cheaper	*arkhas*	December	*kaanoon al-*
cheese	*jubna*		*awwal*
chemist shop	*seidalleeya*	defence	*difaa'*
chief	*ra'ees*	delicious	*ladheedh*
chicken	*dujaaja*	dentist	*tabeeb al-asnaan*
China	*as-seen*	desert	*baadia*
Christian	*maseehee/*	deputy/agent	*wokeel*
	nasraanee		*(wukalaa)*
church	*kaneesa*	Dharaan	*adh-dhahraan*
cigarette	*sagaara*	dictionary	*qaamoos*
	(sagaayer)	diesel oil	*maazoot/ deezil*
cinema	*seenamaa*	difference	
circle	*daa'ira*	between	*farq bane*
city	*madeena*	difficult	*saa'b*
	(mudun)	dinar	*deenaar*
clean	*nodheef*		*(danaaneer)*
clever	*shaatir*	direction	*jiha*
clock/hour	*saa'a*	director	*mudeer*
	(saa'aat)		*(mudara)*
clothing	*libaas*	dirty	*wosakh*
club	*naadee*	distance	*musaafa*
coast	*saahil*	district	*mintaqa*
coffee	*qahwa*		*(manaatiq)*
coffee-house	*maqha*	division (parts)	*qism (aqsaam)*
cold	*baarid*	he did	*amil*
college	*kulleeya*	he is doing	*ya'mal*
colour	*lone (alwaan)*	doctor	*tobeeb*
commerce/trade	*tijaara*	dog	*kalb (kilaab)*
complaint	*shakwa*	Doha	*ad-dawha*
concerning	*bi-khusoos*	dollar	*doolaar*
Congratulations!	*mabrook!*		*(doolaaraat)*
Consulate	*consuleeya*	donkey	*himaar*

door	*baab (ab**waab**)*	explosion	*infijaar*
dress	*libaas*	exports	*saadiraat*
drink	*mash**roob***	external	*khaarijee*
	*(mash**roobaat**)*	eye	*ein (u**yoon**)*
driver	*saa'iq*		
	*(suw**waaq**)*	face	*wajh*
dry	*naa**shif**	family	*aa'ila*
Dubai	*dubei*	far (from)	*ba'eed (min)*
during	*khilaal*	fare (taxi)	*ujra*
dust	*turaab*	fat (adj)	*sameen*
duty	*waajib*	father	*'ab*
	*(waaji**baat**)*		
		feast - at end	*eed al-fitr*
each of	*kul min*	of Ramadan	
early	*bakeer*	feast - of the	*eed al-**adha***
earth/floor/land	*'ard*	sacrifice (Pilgrimage)	
east	*sharq*	February	*shu**baat***
easy	*sahl*	festival	*eed*
he ate	*akal*	few	*qo**leel***
he eats	*yaakul*	film	*film (af**laam**)*
egg	*bay**da (bayd)*	finally	*akhee**ran***
Egypt	*misr*	finger	*usbu' (a**sabi**)*
electricity	*kah**raba***	fire	*naar (fem)*
embassy	*sifaara*	fish	*sam**ak***
employee	*muwadhdhaf*		*(a**smak**)*
	*(mu**wadh**dha**feen**)*	fishing	*sayd as-**samak***
empty	*farrigh*	flag	*'alam*
end	*ni**haa**ya*	flie (coll.)	*dhu**baab***
engineer	*mu**handis***	floor/earth/land	*'ard*
	*(mu**handiseen**)*	floor show	*cab**aaray***
English	*in**gleezee***	it flew	*taar*
envelope	*dharf (dhu**roof**)*	it flies	*yateer*
equipment	*ji**haaz (ajhiza)*	flower	*zahr (zu**hoor**)*
(piece of)		food	*akl*
especially	*khu**soosan***	foot, step	*qadam*
essential	*jaw**haree***		*(aq**daam**)*
evening	*ma**saa'***	for	*li*
evening		forbidden	*mam**noo'***
entertainment	*sahra*	foreign/	*ajnabee*
he entered	*dakhal*	foreigner	*(aja**anib**)*
he enters	*yadkhul*	he forgot	*nasee*
every	*kull*	he forgets	*yansa*
exactly	*ta**maaman***	France	*faransa*
for example	*math**alan***	free	*hurr*
except	*illa*	French	*fran**saawee***
excellent	*mum**taaz***	friend	*so**deeq***
exhibition	*ma'rid*		*(asdi**qaa**)*
it existed	*wajad*	fried/roasted	*maq**lee***
it exists	*yoojad*	from	*min*
exit	*makhraj*	frontier	*hudood*
expense	*mas**roof***	fruit	*fa**waakih***
	*(masaa**reef**)*	fuel oil	*maa**zoot**/dee**zil***
expensive	*ghaalee*	full	*mal**yaan***
experiment	*taj**riba***	future	*mus**taqbal***
	*(taja**arib**)*		
expert (in...)	*kha**beer** (bi...)*	gallon	*gaa**loon***

garment	*thawb*	Royal Highness	**saahib**
	(theeyaab)		*as-sumoo*
gate	*baab (abwaab)*	hire/rent	*eejaar*
he gave	**a'taa**	he hired (from)	*istaa'jar*
he gives	**yaa**tee	he hires (from)	*yasta'jir*
general	*aam*	history	*taareekh*
generous	*kareem*	holiday	**utla**
Germany	*almaaneeya*	honest	*ameen*
gift	*hadeeya*	horizontal	*ufqee*
	(hadaayaa)	horse	*hisaan (husn)*
girl	*bint (banaat)*	hot	*haar*
glad	*farhaan*	hotel	**fun**duq
glass	*kubaaya*		*(fanaadiq)*
(drinking)		hour	**saa'a (saa'aat)**
he went	*raah*	house	*bayt (buyoot)*
he goes	*ya**rooh***	how	*kayf?*
he went in	**dakh**al	how many/	
he goes in	**yad**khul	how much	*kam?*
he went out	**khar**aj	hungry	*jo'aan*
he goes out	**yakh**ruj	hurry (in a)	*musta'jil*
goat	*ma'z*	hunting	*sayd*
God	**allah**	husband	*zawj*
gold	**dha**hab		
golf	*goolf*	ice	*thalj*
good	**teiyyib**	identity card	**huweeya**
government	*hu**koo**ma*	if	*idha*
green	**akh**dar	ill	*mareedh*
group	*jamaa'a*	immediately	**haalan**
guard	**haras**	important	*muhim*
guest	*dhayf (dhuyoof)*	he imported	*istawrad*
guide	*daleel*	he imports	*yastawrid*
guidebook	*kitaab daleel*	imports	*waaridaat*
gulf	*khaleej*	in	*fee*
gun	**midfa'**	incident	*haadith*
	(madaafi')	he informed …	*akhbar*
		(of) (about)	*(bi) ('an)*
hair	**sha'r**	he informs	**yukhbir**
half	*nus*	(of) (about)	*(bi) ('an)*
hand	*yad (aydin)*	India	*al-hind*
handkerchief	*mandeel*	information/	*khabar*
happy	*farhaan*	pl. news	*(akhbaar)*
harbour	*meena*	ink	*hibr*
hard	*sa'b*	inside	**daakhil**
hat	**qubba'a**	international	**dowalee**
head	*ra'as*	invitation	*da'wa*
headcloth	*kafeeyya*	Iran	*eeraan*
head-rope	*'agaal*	Iraq	*al-iraaq*
headquarters	*qeeyaada*	Islam	*al-islaam*
health	**sahha**	island	*jazeera*
heart	*qolb*		*(jazaa'ir)*
heat	*haraara*	Italy	*eetaaliya*
heavy	*thaqeel*		
help (aid)	*'awn*	jacket	**jaakeet**
here	*hina*	January	*kaanoon*
high	*aalee*		*ath-**thaani***
Highness	*sumoo*	Japan	*al-yaabaan*

Jerusalem	al-**quds**	machine	ma**keena**
Jeddah	**jid**da	mad	maj**noon**
Jew, Jewish	ya**hoo**dee	magazine	ma**jalla**
Jews	ya**hood**	man	**raj**ul (**rij**aal)
jewels	ja**waa**hir	manager/	mu**deer**
Jordan	al-**urd**un	director	(muda**raa**)
job	wad**heefa**	Manama	al-ma**naa**ma
journalist	sa**haa**fee	many	**kath**eer
	(sahaafee**yeen**)	map	**khaa**rita/
July	tam**mooz**		kha**reeta**
juice	a**seer**	March	**aadh**aar
June	khuzay**raan**	market	**sooq**
		married	mutaz**ow**wij
kebab	ka**baab**	May	a**yaar**
key	**mif**taah	maybe	**yim**kin
	(mafaa**teeh**)	meat	**lahm**
Khartoum	al-khar**toom**	Mecca	
kilometre	keeloo**mitr**	or Makkah	**makka**
kind	lo**teef**	meeting	ijti**maa'**
king	**mal**ik		(ijtimaa'**aat**)
kingdom	**mam**laka	melon	bot**teekh**
knife	sik**keen**	merchant	**taaj**ir (tuj**jaar**)
he knew	'araf	message	ri**saa**la
he knows	ya'rif		(ra**saa'**il)
knowledge	ilm	messenger	ru**sool**
Kuwait	al-koo**wayt**	metre	**mitr** (am**taar**)
last (adj)	**aa**khir	middle	**wast**
late	muta'**akh**khir	Middle East	ash-**sharq**
lately	a**khee**ran		al-**ows**at
later	baa**dayn**	military (adj)	**ask**aree
law	qaa**noon**	milk	ha**leeb**
	(qawaa**neen**)	million	**mil**yoon
lazy	kas**laan**		(malaa**yeen**)
leader	**qaa**'id	minaret	mi**naa**ra
	(qu**waad**)	minister	wa**zeer**
Lebanon	lub**naan**		(wuza**ra'**a)
left	ya**saar**	ministry	wi**zaa**ra
leg	**rij**l (**arj**ul)	Ministry of…	wi**zaa**rat …
lemon	**lay**moon	Agriculture	az-**zir**aa'a
letter	mak**toob**	Aviation	at-teiyaa**raan**
library	**mak**taba	Commerce	at-ti**jaa**ra
Libya	**lee**biya	Communications	al-muwaasi**laat**
life	**hei**yaa	Education	at-tar**bee**ya
light	**noor**	Defence	ad-di**faa'**
like (adverb)	**mithl**	Development	al-i'**maar**
he liked/		Finance	al-**maa**leeya
loved	**habb**	Foreign Affairs	al-khaari**jee**ya
he likes/loves	ya**hibb**	Health	as-**sahh**a
London	**lan**dan	Industry	as-si**naa'**a
he looked	ta**farr**aj	Interior	ad-daakhi**lee**ya
around		Labour	al-**am**al
he looks		Marine	al-bah**ree**ya
around	yata**farr**aj	Public	as-ashg**haal**
love	**hubb**	Works	al-**aam**ma
lunch	**ghada**	Transport	an-naqlee**yaat**

minute	daqeeqa (daqaa'iq)	old	qodeem
		Oman	umaan
mistake	ghalat (aghlaat)	on	ala
		onions	basal
modern	hadeeth	on the subject of	bi-khusoos
moment	lahdha (lahdhaat)	only	faqat/bass
		open	maftooh
money	faloos	opportunity	fursa
moon	qamr	or	ow
morning	sabaah	oranges (coll.)	burtuqaal
Morocco	al-maghrib	other	aakhar (fem ukhra)
mosque	masjid		
most of	aghlab min	Ottawa	ootaawa
mother	umm	outside	khaarij
mountain	jabal (jibaal)	over	ala/foqe
Mr	seiyid		
much	katheer	pain	waja'
Muharraq	al-muharraq	Palestine	filasteen
Muscat	masqat	paper	woroqa
music	mooseeqa	piece of	(awraaq)
Muslim	muslim (muslimeen)	park	bustaan
		Paris	paarees
		parliament	barlamaan
name	ism (asmaa)	part (of)	juz (ajzaa)
navy	bahreeya	party	hafla
near (to)	qoreeb (min)	political party	hizb (ahzaab)
necessary	dharooree	passenger	raakib (rukkaab)
neighbour	jar (jeeraan)		
never	abadan	passport	jawaaz safar
new	jadeed	past	maadee
news, information	khabar (akhbaar)	the past	al-maadee
		peace	silm
newspaper	jareeda (jaraa'id)	pen	qolum hibr
		pencil	qolum rusaas
New York	niyoo yoork	people (coll.)	naas
night	layl (layaali)	the or a people	ash-sha'b
no	laa	pepper	filfil
noise	sawt	period	mudda
noon	dhuhr	permission/ permit	rukhsa
north	shimaal		
notebook	daftar (dafaatir)	person	shakhs (ashkhaas)
November	tishreen ath-thaanee	petrol	benzeen
		photograph	soora (suwar)
now	alaan	pilgrim	haaj
number	raqm (arqaam)	pilgrimage	hajj
		pills	haboob
October	tishreen al-awwal	place	mahal
		please	minfadlak
office	maktab (makaatib)	police	shurta
		policeman	shurtee
officer	daabit (dubaat)	police station	mahattat ash-shurta
oil (petroleum)	naft	poor	faqeer
oil (vegetable/ lubricating)	zayt	pork	lahm khanzeer
		porter	hammaal

110

possible	*mumkin*	the rest of	*al-baaqee min*
post (mail)	*bareed*	restaurant	*mat'am*
post office	*maktab*	result (of)	*nateeja (min)*
	al-bareed		*(nataa'ij)*
potatoes	*bataata*	he returned	*raja'*
present, current	*haalee*	he returns	*yirja'*
present, gift	*hadeeya*	rice	*ruz*
	(hadaayaa)	rich	*ghanee*
Prime	*ra'ees*	rifle	*bunduqeeya*
Minister	*al-wuzara'*		*(banaadiq)*
press (noun)	*sahaafa*	right (opposite	
press (adj)	*suhufee*	of left)	*yameen*
principal, main	*ra'eesee*	right (correct)	*saheeh*
problem	*mushkila*	river	*nahr*
	(mashaakil)	Riyadh	*ar-reeyaadh*
prophet	*nabee*	room	*ghurfa*
prohibited	*mamnoo'*		*(ghuraf)*
public (adj)	*umoomee*	round (circular)	*mudawwar*
		ruins	*aathaar*
Qatar	*qatar*	ruler	*haakim*
qualification	*salaaheeya*	roasted/fried	*maqlee*
	(salaaheeyaat)	Russia	*rooseeya*
queen	*malika*		
question	*su'aal (as'ila)*	sad	*hazeen*
quickly	*bi-sir'a*	safe (adj)	*saalim*
quiet/calm	*haadee'*	safe (n)	*khazna*
The Quran	*al-quraan*	safety	*salaama*
(The Holy)	*(al-kareem)*	salad	*salaata*
or	*al-quraan*	salt	*milh*
	ash-shareef	Sana'a	*sana'a*
Rabat	*ar-rabaat*	sand	*raml*
rain	*matar*	sandwich	*sandweesh*
Ras Al-Khaima	*ra'as al-khayma*	sauce/gravy	*salsa*
razor blades	*moos hallaaka*	Saudi Arabia	*al-mamlaka*
ready	*haadhir*		*al-arabeeya*
reason	*sabab (asbaab)*		*as-sowdeeya*
recent	*akheer*		
recently	*akheeran*	he said	*qaal*
red	*ahmar*	he says	*yaqool*
Red Sea	*al-bahr*	school	*madrassa*
	al-ahmar		*(madaaris)*
religion	*deen*	sea	*bahr*
rent/hire	*eejaar*	seat (chair)	*kursee*
reply	*jawaab*		*(karaasee)*
	(ajwiba)	secret (noun)	*sirr (asraar)*
repair	*tasleeh*	secret (adj)	*sirree*
report (of	*taqreer*	secretary	*sikriteer*
committee)		he saw	*shaaf*
republic	*jumhureeya*	he sees	*yashoof*
reservation	*hajz*	September	*aylool*
he reserved	*hajaz*	servant	*khaadim*
he reserves	*yahjaz*		*(khuddaam)*
responsible	*mas'ool (an...)*	service	*khidma*
(for...)		at your service	*fee khidmatak*
		Sharjah	*ash-sharja*
responsibility	*mas'ooleeya*	sheep (coll)	*ghanam*
rest (ease)	*raaha*	Sheikh	*shaykh*

111

shirt	*qomees*	tax	*dareeba*
shoes	*ah**dhee**ya*		*(daraa'ib)*
shop	*duk**kaan***	tea	*shei*
	(dakaakeen)	teacher (m)	*mu'allam*
shore	*shatt*	teacher (f)	*mu'allama*
short	*qaseer*	technical	*fannee*
shut	*musakkar*	(adj)	
silver	***fidh**dha*	technique	*fann (funoon)*
simple	*boseet*	telephone	*tilifoon/haatif*
since (time)	*mundh*	temperature	*darajat*
sister	*'ukht*	(heat)	*al-haraara*
slow (adj)	*butee*	tennis	*tennees*
slowly	*bi-**but'***	tent	***khay**ma*
small	*sagheer*		*(khuyoom)*
Smoking	*mam**noo'***	thank you	*shuk**raan**/*
Prohibited	*at-tad**kheen***		*mash**koor**/*
soldier	***ask**aree (askar)*		*ash**koor**ak*
some of	*ba'd min*	there is/are	*fee*
sometimes	*ih**yaan**an*	there is not	*maa fee*
son	*ibn*	there was/were	*kaan fee*
soon (after	*ba'd ka**leel***	that	***dhaa**lik*
a little)		theatre	***mas**rah*
soup	***shoor**ba*	there	*hinaak*
he spoke	*ta**kall**um*	thing	*shee (ashyaa)*
he speaks	*ya**takall**um*	thirsty	*atshaan*
specialist	*ikh**saa'**ee*	this	*haadha*
spectacles	*nad**haar**aat*	thousand	*alf (aalaaf)*
sport	*ree**yaad**ha*	time (period)	*woqt (aw**qaat**)*
square	*marubb'a*	time (occasion)	***murr**a*
stairs	***sull**m*		*(murraat)*
stamp	*taa**bi'***	tired	*taa'baan*
(postage)	*(tawaabi'a)*	to	*ila*
star	*najm (nu**joom**)*	tobacco	***tom**bak*
station	*ma**hatt**a*	today	*al-yome*
step, stage	***dar**aja*	toilet	*hammaam*
stomach	*botn*	tomato	*tamaata*
stone	***ha**jar (ah**jaar**)*	tomorrow	***buk**ra*
street	***shar**ri'*	toothbrush	***fur**sha*
strong	*qowee*		*lil-as**naan***
student	*taalib*	toothpaste	*ma'**joon***
	(tullaab)		*lil-as**naan***
Sudan	*as-soo**daan***	tourism	*see**yaah**a*
sugar	***suk**kar*	tourist	*saa'ih (suyyaah)*
summer	*sayf*	towel	***man**shafa*
sun	*shams*		*(manaa**shif**)*
sweet	***hil**oo*	town	*balad*
he swam	*sabah*	training	*tabreeb*
he swims	***yas**bah*	tree	***sha**jara*
swimming pool	***mas**baha*		*(ash**jaar**)*
Syria	*soo**ree**ya*	tribe	*qo**bee**la*
			(qabaa'il)
table	***taaw**ula*	Tripoli	*ta**raa**bulus*
tailor	*khay**yaat***	trousers	*banta**loon***
target	*hadaf (ah**daaf**)*	true	*saheeh*
he taught	*'allam*	truth	*haqq*
he teaches	*yu'**allam***	Tunisia	***toon**is*

Turkey	*turkeeya*	what?	*aysh?*
type (mark)	*tiraaz*	when?	*aymta/matta?*
		where?	*wayn?/ayn?*
under	*taht*	which?	*ay?*
he understands	*yafham*	while	*baynamaa*
he understood	*fahim*	white	*abyad*
United Arab	*al-imaaraat*	who?	*meen?*
Emirates (The)	*al-arabeeya*	whole	*kull*
	al-mutahida	why?	*laysh?*
university	*jaami'a*	wife	*zawja*
until	*hatta*	wind	*howa*
up	*foqe*	window	*shubbaak*
useful	*mufeed*		*(shabaabeek)*
usual	*aadi*	wine	*nbeedh*
usually	*aadatan*	winter	*shita'*
		with	*ma*
valid, sound	*saalih*	without	*bidoon*
valley	*waadee*	wireless	*laa-silkee*
value	*qeema*	woman	*hurma*
valuable	*thameen*		*(hareem)*
vegetables	*khudra*	word	*kalima*
vertical	*amoodee*		*(kalimaat)*
very	*jiddan*	work	*shogl* or *amal*
village	*qoriya (quraa)*	world	*'aalam*
he visited	*zaar*	he writes	*yaktub*
he visits	*yazoor*	he wrote	*katab*
		writing paper	*woroq al-*
he waited	*intadhar*		*kitaaba*
he waits	*yantadhir*	wrong (n)	*ghalat*
he walked	*mashaa*	wrong (adj)	*ghaltaan*
he walks	*yimshee*		
he wanted	*'araad*	yellow	*asfar*
he wants	*yureed*	Yemen	*al-yaman*
Washington	*waashintun*	yes	*eiwa* or *na'am*
water	*moya* or *maa*	yesterday	*ams*
weak	*da'eef*	young	*sagheer*
weapon	*silaah (asliha)*		
week	*usboo'a*	zero	*sifr*
weather	*taqs*	zoological	*hadeeqat*
weight	*wazn*	gardens	*al-*
west	*gharb*		*heiyawaanaat*

113

NOTES

NOTES